The Styer-Fitzgerald
Program for Functional
Academics

Peer Tutor
Secondary Level
Student Handbook

Created by
CANDICE STYER, Ph.D.
AND
SUZANNE FITZGERALD, M.Ed.

Published by

Specially Designed
Education Services

Styer-Fitzgerald Program for Functional Academics
Peer Tutor Student Handbook

Copyright © 2015, Candice Styer and Suzanne Fitzgerald

First U.S. Edition Published in 2015

SPECIALLY DESIGNED EDUCATION SERVICES
18223 102ND AVE NE
SUITE B
BOTHELL, WA 98011

www.SDESworks.com

ISBN 978-0-9969130-5-8

Cover Design by

www.hewittbydesign.com

A big thank you to our editor extraordinaire, Debbie Austin.

Used by permission from The Styer-Fitzgerald Program for Functional Academics, Secondary Level ©2013 Candice Styer and Suzanne Fitzgerald, Lesson Plans and Data Sheets

Printed by CreateSpace, An Amazon.com Company

CONTENTS

Welcome, Peer Tutor!

Congratulations! You have been accepted as a peer tutor in the
Functional Academics/life skills program. As a peer tutor, you will make a
positive difference in the lives of your peers with disabilities.

Expectations of Peer Tutors

As a peer tutor, you are responsible for your own regular attendance,
positive attitude, ongoing training, teaching, monitoring student
progress, and attending weekly meetings. Here are some details.

Regular Attendance

You will maintain a timesheet to show attendance. Absences are
treated as in other classes (i.e., excused, unexcused, or tardy).

Positive Attitude

As a peer tutor, you are expected to have a positive attitude and to act
in an age-appropriate manner with students in the special education
classroom. Disrespectful or negative behavior is not tolerated.

Ongoing Training

You are expected to participate in a minimum of ___ hours of training
at the beginning of each term. These sessions may be scheduled
before school, during study periods, during lunch, or after school.
Check with the special education teacher.

Teaching

As a peer tutor you will assist with teaching the students in the
Functional Academics or life skills program as they learn social, leisure,
vocational, and academic skills.

Monitoring Student Progress

It is important for you to learn to correctly collect data and to record
each student's progress as you help with individualized programs.

Ask Questions

- Always ask questions! No question is offensive or silly if asked appropriately.

- If a question is specific to a particular student, be sure to ask the teacher or another staff person privately and not in front of other students.

Weekly Meetings

You should plan to meet weekly with the special education teacher. Meetings, lasting about 20 minutes, will be scheduled at a time convenient to both you and the special education teacher. During these meetings you will receive feedback about your students' programs, classroom issues, and your performance as a peer tutor.

Notes

Disability Awareness and Etiquette

Teachers set high standards and expectations for their special education students and the peer tutors who help teach. Here are some things to remember during your service as a peer tutor.

Disability Awareness

It is important to be aware of your peers with disabilities and to learn to interact with them, handling situations with consideration and care.

Interaction

Here are some important things to keep in mind as you interact with special education students.

- Having a disability does not give a special education student an excuse for poor behavior.

- Peer tutors are expected to behave positively and in an age-appropriate manner as they interact with special education students.

- Special education students in the Functional Academics or life skills program are much more like you than they are different. Therefore, as a peer tutor, you should treat each special education student as a peer.

Personal Space

Special education students might inadvertently invade your personal space. Remember that some special education students are unsure how to communicate their feelings and as a result might act inappropriately. For example, a student who likes you or wants your attention might give you a hug and not let go, or grab your hand or arm without asking permission instead of simply talking to you about his or her feelings.

A special education student may also say something that is inappropriate or makes you uncomfortable such as "You are pretty and I love you." It is alright to confront the student and let them know that talking to friends like this is not okay. You could say "I like you, too, but telling people outside of your family that you love them is not okay and it makes people uncomfortable."

If a student enters your personal space, there are ways to respond, depending on the severity of the situation. The following are suggestions for things to say when handling such situations.

- "You are in my personal space and you need to back up."

- "You didn't ask if you could hug me. You need to ask." Even if a special education student asks first, you are not obligated to say "yes." Sometimes, it is good to say "no."

- "This is my space. That is your space. Do not enter my space."

- "You are making me uncomfortable and you need to stop."

- "That is inappropriate. Stop, please."

Although it is rare, sometimes a special education student can become aggressive. If a student becomes agitated, remember the following:

- Say, "I can see you need a minute. I'm going to give you some space." Immediately move away from the student and tell the teacher or a staff person about the situation.

- If you cannot remember what to say, walk away from the student and immediately alert a teacher or staff member.

Helpful Responses

There might be times or situations when you are unsure about how to respond to a special education student. This is not unusual. However, it is important to learn an appropriate response for these possible situations. Before acting or responding, you should ask yourself:

"How will my response help this student in the future?"

How to Communicate

There are many ways that special education students communicate with others, including their peer tutors. Communication can happen through one or more of these ways:

- Verbal

- Tactile

- Sign language

- Modified sign language

- Assistive technology (iPads, switches, computers)

- Facial expressions

- Gestures

- Utterances

- Eye gaze

- Modified "yes" or "no"

- Pictures and picture symbols

STEPS FOR COMMUNICATING

If you do not understand a special education student, do not pretend to do so. Follow these steps:

1. Ask the student to repeat the communication.

2. Say, "I really want to know what you are saying. Please be patient with me and tell me again."

3. If you still do not understand, say, "I still don't understand what you just told me, so I'm going to find a staff person to help me understand."

4. Say, "Thank you for being so patient with me. I really wanted to know what you said."

RULES TO REMEMBER

In cases where you do not understand how or what a special education student is trying to communicate, ask a staff member to tell you. Remember:

- Just because someone cannot speak does not mean he or she does not understand.

- Do not talk about students in front of them unless they are included in the conversation. For example, in front of a student **do not** say, "Why does he make that noise?" Instead, say, "I know you are trying to tell us something, so I am going to try to find out what it is. Does anyone know what it means when ___ makes the _____ noise?"

- It is a very good thing to include non-verbal students in conversations about their communication. It shows that you care and that you want to understand what they are saying.

COMMUNICATING WITH NON-VERBAL STUDENTS

Carrying on a conversation with someone who is non-verbal can be difficult. The special education student might not be able to respond to you in a conventional manner. Here are suggestions:

- Ask a staff person for items or activities the student enjoys.

- Ask the student if there are pictures he or she can share that tell about him or her.

- Ask the teacher for ideas about other topics to talk about.

- Refer to online websites and search video topics for other tips and ideas. For example, you can refer to the peer pages on the Washington Sensory Disabilities Services (WSDS—in Washington State) website at www.wsdsonline.org/video-library/deaf-blind-videos/peer-programs/.

- If it is available in your classroom, ask your teacher for a list of suggested conversational topics and age-appropriate step-by-step social scripts.

Disability Etiquette

WORKING WITH STUDENTS IN WHEELCHAIRS

- To take a student who is in a wheelchair to another location, give a warning before moving him or her. Many special education students have heightened startle reflexes and might be easily upset without first knowing what to expect. Follow these steps:

  1. Tap the student on the shoulder and move to a place where he or she can see and hear you.

  2. Begin with the student's name and say, "_____, we are going to go to _____ now, and I'm going to push you there."

  3. Say, "Are you ready?" or "Here we go."

- If a student is not in his or her wheelchair and you need to move the chair, let the student know what you intend to do and where you will move it.

- **NEVER** hold onto or sit in a student's empty wheelchair—the wheelchair is part of the student's personal space.

WORKING WITH HEARING-IMPAIRED, VISUALLY-IMPAIRED, OR DEAF-BLIND STUDENTS

- If you work with a student who is deaf and has an interpreter, be sure to talk to the student and not to the interpreter.

- If you work with a student who is blind, talk about what is going on around him or her. For example, "Did you hear the door close? Sally Smith just came into the classroom; she's hanging up her coat."

- As you approach someone who has a dual sensory impairment (deaf-blindness), begin by tapping the person on the shoulder. Move your hand down his or her arm until you reach the hand; then give your identifier. Remember, some students with deaf-blindness often have partial hearing and vision. If that is the case, identify yourself verbally or show them your picture so they know who you are. Be sure to check with the teacher to see if the student already has an established greeting.

- When working with students who are deaf-blind, be sure you are putting your hands underneath their hands rather than grabbing the tops of their hands and manipulating them. This method is called "hand-under-hand" and is much less intrusive.

- When you walk with a student who is blind or deaf-blind, offer your arm to him or her. Watch for and warn about changes in the terrain, transition strips, doorways, etc. At all times you must be aware of your surroundings so you can give the student appropriate directions for navigating the environment.

Note: You will want to first check with the teacher to ask if you need further training before walking with a student who is blind or deaf-blind.

Notes

Teaching Methodology

Being a peer tutor is a great way to begin learning good special education teaching habits. This section covers important teaching skills and terms to use and remember when serving as a peer tutor.

Prompting

A prompt is a cue that tells special education students what it is you are asking them to do. In the community setting, the prompt or cue can be the sign at the crosswalk that flashes "Don't Walk." In the classroom during a teaching session, the prompt or cue is the teacher or peer tutor giving an instruction—for example, "Give me $4.99," or "What time is it?"

It is important for you to understand how to use prompts, whether working with students in the classroom or out in the community. You also need to know how to determine when prompts are no longer needed and should be faded.

Prompts during Direct Instruction

When teaching a skill in the classroom (direct instruction):

- Make prompts clear. Tell special education students exactly what you want them to do, for example, "Give me $4.99."

- Vary the prompts so that students learn that a variety of cues have the same meaning. For example, you can say "$4.99" or "That will be $4.99."

Prompts in the Real Environment

When teaching a skill in the community (real environment), you will use prompts or cues that occur without your help in that environment. For example, at a street corner, rather than using a verbal prompt of "Stop," point to the "Walk/Don't Walk" sign and say, "That sign says *Walk*; that means go." Or say, "That sign says *Don't Walk*; that means stop or wait."

Fading Prompts

When you are teaching a new skill, your prompts should be frequent and concise. After a student begins to learn a skill in the real environment, give the student the chance to respond on his or her own before prompting for a response. As students learn a skill, the need for prompts is decreased, thus, you can use prompts less frequently—"fading" them.

You will know you have successfully taught a skill when:

- The student responds to natural cues in the community or environment, such as "Walk/Don't Walk" signs.

- The student responds correctly to prompts in the classroom, regardless of how they are presented (for example whether you say, "$4.99," "Give me $4.99," or "$4.99 please," the response is correct).

Notes

Reinforcement

By reinforcing a correct response or behavior, you are increasing the likelihood of the reoccurrence of that behavior. In other words:

BEHAVIOR > SOMETHING "GOOD" HAPPENS > BEHAVIOR IS LIKELY TO RECUR
(*Reinforcement*)

Types of Reinforcement

It is important to understand that there are different types of reinforcement. You also need to know which reinforcement method is appropriate and when to use it. There are three types of reinforcement: verbal, physical, and tangible.

VERBAL REINFORCEMENT

Verbal reinforcement consists of praise or other words of encouragement. For example, "I like how you are staying on task." Or "You really are working hard!" (See "Pointers for Giving Praise" on page 15.)

PHYSICAL REINFORCEMENT

There are different types of physical reinforcement, and each needs to be age-appropriate. For example, a hug might be appropriate for an elementary-aged student whereas a pat on the back or a "high five" is more natural and acceptable when working with a secondary-aged student.

TANGIBLE REINFORCEMENT

Items that a student can touch or that have value to a special education student can provide tangible reinforcement. Examples of tangible reinforcement can include items such as a paycheck, a token, a '+' on a card, or a certificate of work well done.

Determining the Type of Reinforcement to Use

The appropriate type of reinforcement is often determined by the needs of an individual student or the particular lesson being taught. The type of reinforcement is also often a matter of the preference of an individual tutor or specific special education student. In other words, what works with one student may or may not be effective with another.

You can combine different types of reinforcement. For example, saying "Nice work," while giving a "high five" combines verbal with physical reinforcement.

Frequency of Reinforcement

The frequency of reinforcement is dependent upon where a student is in his or her learning process.

CONTINUOUS REINFORCEMENT

Deliver this method of reinforcement after each and every correct response. Continuous reinforcement is generally used when a student is initially learning a skill.

INTERMITTENT REINFORCEMENT

Deliver this method of reinforcement after a random number of correct responses. Applying intermittent reinforcement is generally used for a student who has learned a skill but still requires feedback about the accuracy of his or her performance.

Delivering Reinforcement

It is vital to the learning process that reinforcement be delivered:

- Immediately
- Clearly
- Frequently

Pointers for Giving Praise

When you praise one of your peer special education students, be specific and encourage the response or behavior you want to see again. Here are some suggestions:

"Nice job...

- paying attention."
- following directions."

- listening to instructions."
- acting like an adult."
- speaking like an adult."
- staying on task."
- working hard."

"I like how you...
- are in your own space."
- are sitting like an adult."
- have your hands and feet to yourself."
- are following directions."
- are listening to directions."
- are trying hard."
- are acting like a high school student."
- are *now* using a quieter tone of voice."

Some Other Words of Praise
- "You're doing a much better job working."
- "That's the way to act like an adult."
- "Thank you for working quietly."
- "I'm so glad you made the right choice."

Notes

_____

_____

_____

_____

_____

_____

_____

_____

_____

_____

_____

_____

_____

_____

_____

_____

_____

_____

_____

_____

_____

_____

_____

_____

_____

_____

_____

Correction Procedures

Using correction procedures appropriately can help increase the skill-levels of special education students as effectively as positive reinforcement does. It is important to use correction procedures so that special education students will learn from their mistakes.

Remember to use correction procedures that are educational rather than harmful to a student's self-esteem.

- Be positive. Avoid saying, "No, that's not right."
- Use steps like those in the following example:
    1. When there is a mistake, say, "Stop" or "Wait," so that the mistake does not continue and become ingrained.
    2. Then say, "Watch me." (Model the behavior, such as: "This is $1.20" and count out the amount.)
    3. Say, "Now you try."
    4. Then reinforce a correct response, such as: "That's right; that is $1.20."

Notes

Summary of Reinforcement and Correction Procedures with Lesson Samples

Remember that:

- When you use reinforcement and correction procedures, both need to be immediate and clear.

- When you give reinforcement, it is the most recent response or behavior that becomes strengthened, especially if that behavior or response is followed with reinforcement in the form of verbal praise.

- Clear and specific praise helps a student understand exactly what he or she has done correctly. For instance, saying "nice job" lets the student know that he did the right thing but does not tell the student what the right thing was. It is better to be specific and say, for example, "Nice job counting out $4.99."

- It might be difficult for you to correct special education students because you do not want to hurt someone's feelings. Be assured, however, that when you use correction procedures appropriately, you are teaching the students you work with—they are learning. When you use clear and appropriate correction procedures, the experience becomes educational rather than ego-deflating for the special education student.

Reinforcement—Lesson Sample

Using reinforcement to teach a skill:

Prompt	Correct Response	Reinforcement
Say, "Give me $4.99."	Student counts out five one-dollar bills.	Say, "Nice job giving me $4.99."

Correction Procedure—Lesson Sample

Using a correction procedure to teach a skill:

Prompt	Response	Correction Procedure
Say, "Give me $4.99."	Student counts, "One, two, four."	When the student makes the mistake, immediately say, "Stop." Repeat the prompt: "$4.99." Say, "Watch me; one, two, three, four, ninety-nine. Now it's your turn."

The correction procedure example shows how the teacher or peer tutor stops the student immediately when the mistake is made or when the number "three" was skipped. Therefore, the student does not learn that four follows two in the sequence. If you do not stop the student at the point of the mistake and he or she keeps counting, the sequence learned is "one, two, four…" rather than "one, two, three, four…"

After stopping the student, you must clearly demonstrate the correct response. For example, "Watch me. This is $4.99" as you count out "one, two, three, four…"

It is natural to want to just say "no," and give the student the correct answer, and then move on to the next trial. However, doing this does not provide the student with the information needed to learn the skill you are trying to teach.

Notes

Data Collection

Data is collected to track student progress and to determine when to move on to the next level of the skill or program.

Teachers use the data to analyze whether to make changes to individual student programs. For example if a student has made little or no progress, it might be time to try a new skill or to break the skill into easier segments. The two methods of data collection most used are:

- Discrete Trial format
- Task Analysis format

Discrete Trial—Recording the Percentage Correct

In the discrete trial data system, you record the correct responses with circles and the incorrect responses with slashes. You are then able to summarize the data by calculating the overall percentage correct over ten to twenty trials of instruction. The dark-edged boxes show the percentage and make a readable "graph" of progress.

Run a minimum of ten trials per day and record for each day that instruction occurs. This is the type of data sheet you will use when teaching skills such as time-telling or counting coins. Here is an example of a discrete trial data sheet with sample data.

Date:	9/1	9/2	9/3								Correct
	10	10	10	10	10	10	10	10	10	10	100%
	9	9	9	9	9	9	9	9	9	9	90%
	8	8	8	8	8	8	8	8	8	8	80%
	7	7	7	7	7	7	7	7	7	7	70%
	6	6	6	6	6	6	6	6	6	6	60%
	5	5	5	5	5	5	5	5	5	5	50%
	4	4	4	4	4	4	4	4	4	4	40%
	3	3	3	3	3	3	3	3	3	3	30%
	2	2	2	2	2	2	2	2	2	2	20%
	1	1	1	1	1	1	1	1	1	1	10%

Prompt: "Give me _____."

Task Analysis—Recording the Number of Prompts

Use the task analysis format to count the number of prompts per step in the process required for a student to perform a particular task or skill. You will teach the skill and record the number of prompts per step until the student can perform the entire task independently.

If a student has difficulty with a particular step, you need to break the task into smaller/simpler steps until the student can perform the task independently. A task analysis is the type of data sheet you will use when you teach skills in the community such as street crossing and grocery shopping.

The following is an example of a task analysis data sheet.

Task Analysis	Initials: AB	Initials: AB	Initials:	Initials:
	Date: 9/1	Date: 9/4	Date:	Date:
	Prompts	Prompts	Prompts	Prompts
1 Finds nearest bus stop	//	/		
2 Finds bus number	/	/		
3 Gets on correct bus	//	//		
4 Pays/shows pass	/	/		
5 Finds a seat	//	/		
6 Pulls cord prior to stop	/	/		
7 Exits the bus	/	/		
Total Number of Prompts	10	8		
Bus Stop Location	3rd & Main	B Street		
Final Destination	17th St.	J Street		

Accuracy in Data Collection

It is important to understand that you are not "being mean" when you mark responses as incorrect. The rule is: If reinforcing a student's response, the response is marked as correct. However, if you were required to do a correction procedure, the response is marked as incorrect even if the student goes on to respond accurately after having been corrected.

The following diagram illustrates the rule of when to record a response as correct or incorrect.

Prompt ➝ Correct Response ➝ Reinforcement (draw a circle on discrete trial data sheet)

Prompt ➝ Incorrect Response ➝ Correction Procedure (draw a slash on discrete trial data sheet and a hash mark on task analysis data sheets)

Notes

Grade Requirements

To Maintain an "A"

- Spend time with a special education student, three times a term, outside of class time. This can be done in school settings.

- Keep a weekly record using "My Peer Tutor Journal" found in the back of this Handbook. Write about your experiences as a peer tutor working with special education students. Turn in the journal at least three times per semester. The first due date is _____.

- Educate at least one of your peers about disabilities. Explain to the special education teacher how you accomplished this.

To Maintain a "B"

- Spend time with a special education student, two times a term, outside of class time.

- Keep a weekly record using "My Peer Tutor Journal" found in the back of this Handbook. Write about your experiences as a peer tutor working with special education students. Turn in the journal at least three times per semester. The first due date is _____.

- Educate at least one of your peers about disabilities. Explain to the special education teacher how you accomplished this.

To Maintain a "C"

- Work with special education students in class.

- Keep a weekly record using "My Peer Tutor Journal" found in the back of this Handbook. Write about your experiences as a peer tutor working with special education students. Turn in the journal at least three times per semester. The first due date is _____.

- Educate at least one of your peers about disabilities. Explain to the special education teacher how you accomplished this.

> *When asked what he'd gained from his peer tutor experience, Joel said, "A bunch of great friends and life experiences I will never forget."*
>
> *Amanda said, "I became a peer tutor because I've always wanted to work in the special education field and I wanted to gain experience and joy from working with great kids."*

▌Weekly Planner　　SEPTEMBER
WEEK 1

Monday
_____

Tuesday
_____

Wednesday
_____

Thursday
_____

Friday
_____

WEEK 2

Monday
_____

Tuesday
_____

Wednesday
_____

Thursday
_____

Friday
_____

WEEK 3

Monday
_____
_____
_____

Tuesday
_____
_____
_____

Wednesday
_____
_____
_____

Thursday
_____
_____
_____

Friday
_____
_____
_____

WEEK 4

Monday
_____
_____
_____

Tuesday
_____
_____
_____

Wednesday
_____
_____
_____

Thursday
_____
_____
_____

Friday
_____
_____
_____

OCTOBER

WEEK 1

Monday

Tuesday

Wednesday

Thursday

Friday

WEEK 2

Monday

Tuesday

Wednesday

Thursday

Friday

WEEK 3

Monday

_____

_____

_____

Tuesday

_____

_____

_____

Wednesday

_____

_____

_____

Thursday

_____

_____

_____

Friday

_____

_____

_____

WEEK 4

Monday

_____

_____

_____

Tuesday

_____

_____

_____

Wednesday

_____

_____

_____

Thursday

_____

_____

_____

Friday

_____

_____

_____

NOVEMBER

WEEK 1

Monday

_____

Tuesday

_____

Wednesday

_____

Thursday

_____

Friday

_____

WEEK 2

Monday

_____

Tuesday

_____

Wednesday

_____

Thursday

_____

Friday

_____

WEEK 3

Monday
_____
_____
_____

Tuesday
_____
_____
_____

Wednesday
_____
_____
_____

Thursday
_____
_____
_____

Friday
_____
_____
_____

WEEK 4

Monday
_____
_____
_____

Tuesday
_____
_____
_____

Wednesday
_____
_____
_____

Thursday
_____
_____
_____

Friday
_____
_____
_____

DECEMBER

WEEK 1

Monday
_____
_____
_____

Tuesday
_____
_____
_____

Wednesday
_____
_____
_____

Thursday
_____
_____
_____

Friday
_____
_____
_____

WEEK 2

Monday
_____
_____
_____

Tuesday
_____
_____
_____

Wednesday
_____
_____
_____

Thursday
_____
_____
_____

Friday
_____
_____
_____

WEEK 3

Monday
_____
_____
_____

Tuesday
_____
_____
_____

Wednesday
_____
_____
_____

Thursday
_____
_____
_____

Friday
_____
_____
_____

WEEK 4

Monday
_____
_____
_____

Tuesday
_____
_____
_____

Wednesday
_____
_____
_____

Thursday
_____
_____
_____

Friday
_____
_____
_____

JANUARY

WEEK 1

Monday
_____

Tuesday
_____

Wednesday
_____

Thursday
_____

Friday
_____

WEEK 2

Monday
_____

Tuesday
_____

Wednesday
_____

Thursday
_____

Friday
_____

WEEK 3

Monday
_____
_____
_____

Tuesday
_____
_____
_____

Wednesday
_____
_____
_____

Thursday
_____
_____
_____

Friday
_____
_____
_____

WEEK 4

Monday
_____
_____
_____

Tuesday
_____
_____
_____

Wednesday
_____
_____
_____

Thursday
_____
_____
_____

Friday
_____
_____
_____

FEBRUARY

WEEK 1

Monday

_____

Tuesday

_____

Wednesday

_____

Thursday

_____

Friday

_____

WEEK 2

Monday

_____

Tuesday

_____

Wednesday

_____

Thursday

_____

Friday

_____

WEEK 3

Monday
_____
_____
_____

Tuesday
_____
_____
_____

Wednesday
_____
_____
_____

Thursday
_____
_____
_____

Friday
_____
_____
_____

WEEK 4

Monday
_____
_____
_____

Tuesday
_____
_____
_____

Wednesday
_____
_____
_____

Thursday
_____
_____
_____

Friday
_____
_____
_____

MARCH

WEEK 1

Monday
_____
_____
_____

Tuesday
_____
_____
_____

Wednesday
_____
_____
_____

Thursday
_____
_____
_____

Friday
_____
_____
_____

WEEK 2

Monday
_____
_____
_____

Tuesday
_____
_____
_____

Wednesday
_____
_____
_____

Thursday
_____
_____
_____

Friday
_____
_____
_____

WEEK 3

Monday

Tuesday

Wednesday

Thursday

Friday

WEEK 4

Monday

Tuesday

Wednesday

Thursday

Friday

APRIL

WEEK 1

Monday

_____

Tuesday

_____

Wednesday

_____

Thursday

_____

Friday

_____

WEEK 2

Monday

_____

Tuesday

_____

Wednesday

_____

Thursday

_____

Friday

_____

WEEK 3

Monday
_____

Tuesday
_____

Wednesday
_____

Thursday
_____

Friday
_____

WEEK 4

Monday
_____

Tuesday
_____

Wednesday
_____

Thursday
_____

Friday
_____

MAY

WEEK 1

Monday
_____
_____
_____

Tuesday
_____
_____
_____

Wednesday
_____
_____
_____

Thursday
_____
_____
_____

Friday
_____
_____
_____

WEEK 2

Monday
_____
_____
_____

Tuesday
_____
_____
_____

Wednesday
_____
_____
_____

Thursday
_____
_____
_____

Friday
_____
_____
_____

WEEK 3

Monday

_____
_____
_____

Tuesday

_____
_____
_____

Wednesday

_____
_____
_____

Thursday

_____
_____
_____

Friday

_____
_____
_____

WEEK 4

Monday

_____
_____
_____

Tuesday

_____
_____
_____

Wednesday

_____
_____
_____

Thursday

_____
_____
_____

Friday

_____
_____

JUNE

WEEK 1

Monday
_____
_____
_____

Tuesday
_____
_____
_____

Wednesday
_____
_____
_____

Thursday
_____
_____
_____

Friday
_____
_____
_____

WEEK 2

Monday
_____
_____
_____

Tuesday
_____
_____
_____

Wednesday
_____
_____
_____

Thursday
_____
_____
_____

Friday
_____
_____
_____

WEEK 3

Monday

_____
_____
_____

Tuesday

_____
_____
_____

Wednesday

_____
_____
_____

Thursday

_____
_____
_____

Friday

_____
_____
_____

WEEK 4

Monday

_____
_____
_____

Tuesday

_____
_____
_____

Wednesday

_____
_____
_____

Thursday

_____
_____
_____

Friday

_____
_____
_____

My Peer Tutor Journal

Date: _____

_____

_____

_____

_____

_____

Date: _____

_____

_____

_____

_____

_____

Date: _____

_____

_____

_____

_____

_____

Date: _____

_____

_____

_____

_____

_____

Date:

_____

_____

_____

_____

_____

Date:

_____

_____

_____

_____

_____

Date:

_____

_____

_____

_____

_____

Date:

_____

_____

_____

_____

_____

Date: _____

_____

_____

_____

_____

_____

_____

Date: _____

_____

_____

_____

_____

_____

_____

Date: _____

_____

_____

_____

_____

_____

_____

Date: _____

_____

_____

_____

_____

_____

_____

Date:

_____

_____

_____

_____

_____

_____

Date:

_____

_____

_____

_____

_____

_____

Date:

_____

_____

_____

_____

_____

_____

Date:

_____

_____

_____

_____

_____

_____

Date:

_____

_____

_____

_____

_____

_____

Date:

_____

_____

_____

_____

_____

_____

Date:

_____

_____

_____

_____

_____

_____

Date:

_____

_____

_____

_____

_____

Date:

_____

_____

_____

_____

_____

Date:

_____

_____

_____

_____

_____

Date:

_____

_____

_____

_____

_____

Date:

_____

_____

_____

_____

_____

Date:
_____
_____
_____
_____
_____
_____

Date:
_____
_____
_____
_____
_____
_____

Date:
_____
_____
_____
_____
_____
_____

Date:
_____
_____
_____
_____
_____
_____

Date:

Date:

Date:

Date:

Date:

_____

_____

_____

_____

_____

_____

Date:

_____

_____

_____

_____

_____

_____

Date:

_____

_____

_____

_____

_____

_____

Date:

_____

_____

_____

_____

_____

_____

Date: _____

_____

_____

_____

_____

_____

Date: _____

_____

_____

_____

_____

_____

Date: _____

_____

_____

_____

_____

_____

Date: _____

_____

_____

_____

_____

_____

Made in the USA
Monee, IL
22 July 2023

39564018R00036